SECOND SIGHT

SECOND SIGHT

poems

Stacie Smith

June Campbell Rose

Shanti Arts Publishing
Brunswick, Maine

SECOND SIGHT
Poems

Copyright © 2020 Stacie Smith and June Campbell Rose

All Rights Reserved
No part of this book may be used or reproduced
in any manner whatsoever without written
permission from the publisher.

Published by Shanti Arts Publishing
Interior and cover design by Shanti Arts Designs

Shanti Arts LLC
193 Hillside Road
Brunswick, Maine 04011

shantiarts.com

Cover photograph by Stacie Smith, *June and Nathan*,
1967. Photographs on pages 16 and 52 by Stacie
Smith; photographs on pages 34 and 70 by June
Campbell Rose. All images used with permission.

Printed in the United States of America

ISBN: 978-1-951651-17-6 (softcover)

Library of Congress Control Number: 2020935780

For our grandchildren
Ari, Saeran, Ivory, Devyn,
Grace, Rose, Kolton, Ryder

and for all grandchildren everywhere

Let this darkness be a bell tower and you the bell.
　　　　　　　　　　　~Rainer Maria Rilke

CONTENTS

AN UNCOMMON COLLABORATION — 13

STACIE SMITH

PLAYA SERIES X	16
THIS ENORMITY	17
CRICKETS	18
MUSE'S WHISKERS	19
MARY'S PICTURES	20
YAQUINA BAY II	21
MONDAY	22
STUCK	23
ONE WORD	24
WAKING DREAM	25
SALMON RIVER ESTUARY	26
ABIQUIU WIND	27
AGAIN	28
DRIFTER	29
SMALL BOOK SERIES V	30
WHAT TO DO WHILE THE RIVER RISES	31

JUNE CAMPBELL ROSE

SMALL WORDS	34
SCARECROW	35
SYMPHONY	36
OUTLANDER	37
SECOND SIGHT	38
INTUITION	39
THROUGH A WINDOW	40
BRAIN WASH	41
THOUGHT EXCHANGE	42
OLSEN HOUSE	43
MOMENT OF SILENCE	44
THE 12th OF NEVER	45
THOSE WHO PUBLISH PEACE	46
ALTER-EGO	47
KINDRED SOULS	48
BALLOONS	49

Stacie Smith

NEW WAVE	52
FINGERLINGS	53
HERE	54
COTTONWOOD	55
HOMESTEAD PERSIAN	56
SOMETHING RISING UP	57
THE COLOR OF SNOW	58
FINDING WHAT IS LEFT	59
MONASTERY THE WORLD	60
WINTER OF THE WORLD	61
FALLING	62
CONFLUENCE	63
BENEFICIARY	64
EMILY	65
DEPARTURE	66
OPEN LETTER TO THE DECEASED	67

June Campbell Rose

TIDAL POOL AHA	70
NATURAL GRACE	71
MONARCH DAY	72
REMEDIAL TEARS	73
ODE TO AN EARTHEN VESSEL	74
UNEXPECTED GREEN	75
OCTOBER FIRST	76
FALL EQUINOX	77
JANUARY MORNING	78
SNOW PLOW FANTASY	79
OLD SAGE	80
SOMETIMES THE MOON	81
MY FACE, A GLOBE	82
AUTUMNAL PSALM	83
DEPARTURE	84
HEBREWS 11:5	85

ACKNOWLEDGMENTS

Grateful acknowledgment is made to the editors of the following publications where these poems were first published:

Fireweed: "Stuck," "Finding What is Left"

Meanwhile the Earth: Poems from Cougar Creek: "Open Letter to the Deceased: Cougar Creek Series XXIX"

Open Burning: "Crickets," "Salmon River Estuary," "Beneficiary," "Emily"

Real News: "Monday," "Again," "The Color of Snow," "Departure"

West Wind Review: "Monastery the World"

AN UNCOMMON COLLABORATION

June and Stacie first met in 1967 in East Boothbay, Maine, in what turned out to be an important juncture for these two kindred souls. Stacie and a companion had traveled from Eugene, Oregon, to Portland, Maine, lured by this area's tradition for making wooden sailboats. By chance, they found the Boothbay peninsula and a cluster of boatyards in this quaint village located between a mill pond and the Damariscotta River.

June had recently given birth to her first son, Nathan. Stacie was a photographer and poet who met this mother and child at the post office and wanted to take their portrait. This turned out to be a very special meeting during which time a bond was made: both were born-again poets who kept journals and notebooks, filled with their thoughts laid down, like life lines to a deeper self.

Other similar histories include sharing Aries as a birth sign; remembering first poems written at the age of twelve; and having fathers who were florists, which might explain their great love for nature and conservation. Later in life, both were the mothers of three sons, and throughout a fifty-year time spread, their communication of letters, poems, and phone calls became a link of ongoing exchange, defying distance and still pursuing the love of words to explain life's complexities and ponder unanswerable questions.

Along with the onset of the internet came the accessibility of email and a more efficient way to share their thoughts. This technology proved useful early in 2019 when Stacie discovered June's manila envelope filled with some of her poems from the 1980s. She immediately sent the titles and a few of the poems to June via email asking, "Do you remember these?" Shortly after this, June began a serious search for her older poems and found a manila envelope dated November 1984, which contained a collection of Stacie's poems.

The fact that these two discoveries happened almost simultaneously gave Stacie an idea which may have been brewing for a long time: the possibility of a unique collaboration between two poets whose histories include deep roots upon opposite shores, a chance meeting, and the exchange of poems, spanning time and distance to materialize now in this book, fifty years in the making.

STACIE SMITH

PLAYA SERIES X

There was something
no one knew
because it just
could not be said.

That bothered me
so I moved west
lured by the myth
of new beginnings.

Mining for new words
to say what can't be said,
I looked and looked
and looked, and didn't find

but I found you, and
where our paths converged
new ways to try to say
what can't be said emerged.

THIS ENORMITY

The numinous mundane
plays hide and seek
inside an ordinary day.

Epic stories hide in every face
and there's a world of innuendo
in a single random glance.

Somewhere someone turns a page—
another mystery unfolds.
Today will be tomorrow soon enough

and yesterday is nothing but a dream.
There's a word for it, this wild enormity—
it glimmers in and out of sight

and leaves a trail of riddles
as it moseys through the darkness
toward the light.

CRICKETS

Crickets trill all night long
nourishing the darkness where I live
so why should I labor to tell you
my real name when it would not
even feed a snake?

The coyotes have moved deeper
into the hills but the crickets stay
saying over and over again
"It is real! It is real!
It is real!"

MUSE'S WHISKERS

After illness
I see differently
as if my eyes are
coming back to life
but with a heightened
sensitivity to light
after being burned
by days and nights
of fever dreams.
      Look:
Boots on the stoop.
Ice on fallen leaves.
My breath a frosty cloud
that hovers on the air
then dissipates
and over there
the orange cat
nonchalant
her whiskers glinting
in the frigid sun.

MARY'S PICTURES

"They come to me in dreams," she says,
"these images of Universe. Look!
This turtle is a cosmic hub, spitting stars.
This branch becomes a snake!"
The neighbors watch. They say
"What sense is there to make of it,
this branch becoming snake?
If images like these can come to her in sleep,
just think what she might do, awake!"

YAQUINA BAY II

Sunrise—
is that all it is,
this unmitigated light,
this ruby radiance?
Is this how it is
to be swept into
that next eventuality?
Simply daybreak
shining through
my open door?

MONDAY

While hanging out the wash
I notice my strong eye seeing
the flap and billow of damp,
functional color,
each clothespin a good deed.
Now the pajamas will dry,
the towels will bleach and sweeten
in the wind, each wooden pin
an alleluia in the August sun.
My weak eye, mind's eye,
sees something else.
Here, no usefulness,
no object but delight exists,
nothing linear or fixed
on which to clip the things
I think I need.
And when my two eyes focus
to function as one
I see the day as it is,
shining in the washday sun.

STUCK

Stuck in these hills
by my own design
I find pathways
to the other world
choked with introspection now.

This cabin full of comfort,
hand-made home-spun
comfrey poultice atrophy
has put my wits to sleep
and I am weak
from these holistic ways.

I need to touch
the rotting urban stones
and breathe the sickened air.
These quiet, clean
and sun-filled days
are bad for me.

ONE WORD

Despite all my casting and waiting
not one word has taken the bait
so I reel in my line and call it a day.
If a poem wants to come, it will.
Who am I anyway, to think a fish
would take my little hook?

Back home and hungry
I put a skillet on the stove.
Dreaming of rainbow trout
I crack an egg instead.
Nothing to be done.
The holy is everywhere.

WAKING DREAM

This waking dream
of golden hands
unfolding me—
what is it
they wish to know?
And how can I say it
when all my life
I've been mute?
How can I say it—
this soft thing,
this tender shoot,
this waking dream
of golden hands
unfolding me?

SALMON RIVER ESTUARY

Great Blue Heron
stands so still so long

then in a flash
spears its silvery prey.

Two women laugh
in a red canoe.

Low fog rolls over the dune.
Men in a boat cast their lines.

I watch from the bank
of the Salmon River.

Some say this all could end
but I'm not so sure.

These stones, this air,
this water and this sun

know so much more
than I.

ABIQUIU WIND

At first I thought it was a voice,
someone far away, singing the word *love*
but it was just the Abiquiu wind.

In this high wild and lonesome it's easy
to mistake the wind for a lover's croon.

Up here sometimes it's hard to tell—
love-cry or the foretelling of a storm?

I have no clue. But I swear I heard
a song I knew and loved when I was young—
      "my one and only you"

AGAIN
Monroe Street Series I

I woke up grateful for this day
with bread and poems in it.
Oh, I know the news is bad
and certain men behave
as if they own the world
but evidence abounds
that everyone who's born
will someday lose it all

and kindness rises
every morning with the sun
and goes to work to bake the bread
while in another part of town
a poet notices the slant of light
and putting pen to page
begins again to try
to set things right.

DRIFTER

this aimlessness
kicks up
a thirst
no wine
can satisfy
i try to be
at ease
in my own skin
i try
but mostly
it's the road
that soothes
by its unfolding
shows me
there's no need
to know
which way
to go

SMALL BOOK SERIES V

Belly laughing
with an old friend,
I feel restored—
nothing to reveal,
nothing to hide.
You tell me your name,
I'll tell you mine.
We already know
the punch line!

WHAT TO DO WHILE THE RIVER RISES

Study the phases of the moon.
Practice the Australian Crawl.
Say please and thank you.
Go off trail.
Question assumptions.
Do the laundry.
Learn to float.
Dance on the head of a pin.

Make soup.
Remember to breathe.
Talk to a friend.
Pay attention to dreams.
Explore high ground.
Feed the cat.
Stay in tune with the news.
Blame no one.

JUNE CAMPBELL ROSE

SMALL WORDS

I'm for
small words
that have lost a voice—
the tall hat, soft shoe, velvet kind,
flattened out in trunks,
adjusted to the times,
in need of being found.

Not for the dark
or singing alone,
their grace is grown
by getting out and around again,
as joy is easy
between friends,
power comes afresh:
  a surprise twist of timing
    a sweet twirl of sequence
      a flash of silk lining—
    and back comes
  that old song and dance
  of a new shining.

SCARECROW

Waist deep
in a garden of weeds,
she is anything
but scared.
In fact, her countenance exceeds
any act of watchfulness;
she radiates her smile
ever westward,
rain or shine—
a lesson for my
windowed soul—
to strike a joyful pose
and know
the will to survive
is sometimes gained
just by
standing still.

SYMPHONY

Beside my porch,
crickets in a field
sing the treble tone
of a long prelude.
Nothing moves
in the predawn glow.

A distant roar of surf
pounds out the bass
rolling in at Ocean Point;
and somewhere—between
the near and far—

I hear the notes
of an alto voice:
the mourning dove's
soft exit song
as molecules
of pooling light
    begin
        to
            dance.

OUTLANDER
a post-partum poem

Too soon after
the long jolt
of transition,
I am startled
by morning,
and the clothes line
is a cold splinter
in the sun.

Still fresh from
the swift exchange
for an empty womb,
I am unfamiliar
and bewildered by
soap-sud prisms
on the sill.

Minutes beyond
the triggered shift
from random fancy
to the bright ice
of wet sheets,
I am a spectator,
sniffing in the wind
for a friendly scent.

SECOND SIGHT

Not surprised
that love
has substance,
she sets dreams visible.
The unlike stuff
of heart and hand agree
for she measures
food and faith
in one cup.

Such an easy sight
that hugs two worlds,
  gives body to
  ethereal flow;
 a work of light
 brought home,
  wrapped
in human terms.

INTUITION

is a ruby moment
set upon
the purple darks
of lidded sight

a quick slant
of reddened light
throws its bright shadow
on my startled

agreement

THROUGH A WINDOW

A scene of random,
humble acts:

rings of coffee stains,
a used brush,
soiled socks
dropped on the floor,
scribbled words
hastily written—"gone to town"—
endearing signs
of one's careless race
with time:
sweet moments
of selfhood,
left
behind

BRAIN WASH

Today
the words
in my head
are an overload
of work clothes
soaking
in a tub:
cloudy
thoughts
in a swirl
of suds
too fractional
  to be
    told—

THOUGHT EXCHANGE

For what purpose—
this war of words
with no saving grace—
    shaking up
my comfort zone?

A wake-up call, perhaps—
but nothing to die for.

Sweep the floor,
take out the trash,
put some flowers
on the mantel,
write this poem
and call it good.

OLSEN HOUSE

I've been here before—
a specter, wake-sleeping,
reading cracks
on the floor—like a map.

I know this gospel of light—
how the vanishing point
signals a passageway,
drawing the artist home.

MOMENT OF SILENCE

This afternoon bliss
is better kept
unlettered.
It simply exists—
slowly poised
as sailboats,
wing and wing—
creep past this
moment of sundown
while all that floats
on mooring lines
point the other way

but I find it singing
the essential reply
of wordless prayer—
at once, fulfilled
and rightly posed,
the whole is still—
  becalmed
    and
      unaware.

THE 12TH OF NEVER

The song says
"forever is a long, long time"
yet time is not
clock-wise.

Human calculations
are but dots of variables
adrift on an ocean
of educated guesses
floating in a galaxy
of All That Is.

THOSE WHO PUBLISH PEACE

What rarity—
　your natural gift
　for cures
　that finds no fault,
　but acts upon
　swift remedy
　to rightly bind
　my humankind.
How beautiful—
　your sleight
　of hand
　that doesn't pry,
　but slips an answer
　under the door
　and waits
　for no reply.

ALTER-EGO

He was the unreal
part of me
that ran quick circles
when I had lines
to measure out
and
He was my second wind
for long
going straight
when I had squares
to occupy

KINDRED SOULS

Like mine,
a pattern of the stars
slipped Aries
into place
for your birth;

between us,
a whole world
and yet,
a mirror of timing
gives reflection
to our likeness now.

Met again,
our eyes transmit
a link of affection
a shining script
of mutual light
tells us
how
we're doing.

BALLOONS

Going up,
they trace the whimsy
of random flight—
meltaway dots
of festal escape,
they fade, mid-sky,
trailing threads
of mortality.

How easily
they disappear
into the cosmic mind—
like angels dancing
on the head
of a pin,
pointing out infinity
as we lose count.

STACIE SMITH

NEW WAVE

Each new wave
collides with shore
in its own way—
this one tickles
the stony headland
then retreats,
shushing as it goes.
The next one strikes
with such velocity
it shakes the very air.
Here comes one
flinging wind-drift
and a spectrum
of unnamable greys
ephemeral as smoke
or mist or thought.
So—this is how
the ocean breathes!

FINGERLINGS
Cougar Creek Series XLV

Coho fingerlings in Cougar Creek
the very color of where they live
invisible when motionless
but when they dart for cover
toward the shade of overhanging ferns
their flashing shadows for an instant
make them manifest.

Last winter when the aged Coho spawned
the creek ran fast and full but now
in summer flow has slowed, creating
shallow beds and tiny waterfalls and
little eddies and cascades and riffles
where surviving progeny can practice
what their parents knew.

Later when the time is right
as if in thrall to ancient ritual
the young will swim toward the sea
where they may grow in strength
and cunning as they learn to stay alive
to find their way toward the source
of their beginning.

HERE

This blank page—
a beckon to the fleeting word,
a net to snare the metamorphic thought,
the butterfly word,
not to pin it down
but to let it take my breath away.

Look: azure, crimson, gold—
its wings flutter
like my thoughts do,
alighting here and there
and here again, here
where the nectar is.

COTTONWOOD

Today the cottonwood
had no answers for me
when I sat wondering,
and wind shook the leaves
and sun shone through grasses
with crowns of radiant seed
and birds sang uncomplicated songs.

It can be a sweet thing
when the day has no replies
and questions blow in the wind
like so much dust,
and tears of unknowing
fall to the thirsty ground
like rain.

HOMESTEAD PERSIAN

Whoever wove this rug
knew the heart of symmetry,
allowed the flaws
as part of pattern too.
Each blunder soon or later
found its match.
In full control, the weaver
wove this motley swath
and knew how come.

SOMETHING RISING UP

There is something rising up
easy and sure as jonquils every spring
pushing up through the cold hard ground.

Some fierce knowing is rising up
steady and bold as a seed
taking root in the stony field.

There is something rising up,
tears from the heart's great sky
falling down and down like angry rain.

THE COLOR OF SNOW
   for Carolyn

It's only a prayer,
this feeling that starts
at the break of day.
Birds head south
in dark flocks
or in pairs or alone,
stranding us here
bereft of their songs
while the grey settles in
and the prayer hurts all day
like a bruise on a bone.
I only know what I see—
leaves the color of blood
blanket the ground.
Breath-clouds
the color of snow
hover, then disappear.

FINDING WHAT IS LEFT

The way time goes
I turn my head
and trees are turning gold.
I hear a note of panic
in the jay's cry
and watch the urgent motions
of the gatherers of seed.
One breath of days ago
the season brought me
all I needed; warmth and color,
clarity and ripened fruit.
Now so soon,
the branches clatter
in a cooling wind.
Creatures all around me
heed the urge to dig
and grow fat.
I feel the pressure too,
to gather and store up,
but I squander these fading days
instead, finding what is left
of what is bright,
feeding my mind's eye,
making it fat with color.
My spirit like a squirrel's cheek
stuffed with a load of light
because of winter.

MONASTERY THE WORLD

This cell, the day as it is,
an enclosure of simple facts.
Moths at the window,
oats in a bowl.
Moments awash
in what is real.

This cloister,
habitat of the mundane.
Sodden mornings,
shoes on the stoop.
Transcendence tangled
in the anchor line.

This monastery, the world,
place of last resort.
I petitioned for this
in naïve prayer, remember?
Motes in the sun shaft,
silence that sings.

WINTER OF THE WORLD

I want to go home
but the roads are closed.
Debris from a life
of wild weather
chokes the interstate
grinding all agenda
to a halt.

What happens when
so much silence falls
so suddenly? Who am I
when stopped in my tracks
by circumstances beyond
my control?

It's come to this—
paralyzed, mute,
nowhere to go until
the plowman comes
to deliver me. Deliver me
from this winter
of the world.

FALLING

Since no one is there to hear,
a tree falls without a sound.
At least that's what they say.
Even so, I hear it in my mind,
that big old cedar crashing
as it crushes any upright thing
standing in its downward way.

Meanwhile unseen
I walk to the market
for bread and wine.
No one hears me go.

Old age has its benefits—
the pleasure of transparency,
the freedom of not being heard,
the rush that comes from yielding
to the pull of gravity at last,
the readiness to fall, invisible,
without a sound.

CONFLUENCE
Little River / White Creek

Do planets dream?
I think so.
Sometimes I dream
I am orbited by moons.
Icy moons shine blue light on me
causing my breath to create tides.

Can this be true?
Creatures spawn in my blood.
My hair is the grass
where spiders breed and weave nets
where winged beasts come to die.

I dreamed I had come here to die
but the raucous cry of the crow
awoke me, the planet beneath me
stirring from a dream about moons
and the unearthly light
exuded by stones and trees
when no one is there to see.

BENEFICIARY

Precious objects—
try as I might to divest myself
now look: the candlestick,
the shells she gathered one by one.

I like to travel fast
but look: the rocking chair,
the quilt, the lamp,
the myrtle bowl.

I want to travel light
but look: the cast-iron pan,
the cutting board he made,
the stoneware jug, the spoons.

I try to travel free
of the burden of things
but look: the scroll, the cups,
the ancestral bones.

EMILY

I want to visit Emily
but she's long gone.
At least that's what they say.
I think she's still alive.
We just don't see.

I've heard her called "Vesuvius."
I want to know that fire.
I'll open up my door
and ask her in although it's said
she's very shy.

Some say she shut her door
against the world
but I say absolutely not. I say
she opened to a vaster place
the rest of us forgot.

DEPARTURE

Approaching the runway
the jet in my dream
revved and roared,
rolled faster and faster
then surged and lifted
as its landing gear
folded into place.
Then it banked smoothly
up and over the town
I once called home.
When finally fully aloft
I looked down
at what had been—
a dream within a dream.

No one told me
it would be like this—
departure, I mean—
so easy, so swift,
so out of this world.
I don't remember
booking this trip
but here I am,
miles high, at the mercy
of mystery, winging it,
all things once familiar
now dovetailing
dream into dream
into dream.

OPEN LETTER TO THE DECEASED
Cougar Creek Series XXIX

Maybe from where you are—
if you are anywhere
or nowhere or who knows, everywhere—
some light from that place
might rain down on us or shine or fall
or somehow help us out here
stuck as we are in this web
of unknowing.

I thought about you
as I walked the creek-side trail
to the Buddha who now wears
a crown and cloak of moss.
I wondered how you are—
if you are anything
or nothing or who knows—
everything.

  —for Jack

JUNE CAMPBELL ROSE

TIDAL POOL AHA

Lukewarm habitat
and scarcity
sends the population
fleeing.
Silver-side up
and frantic upon
the high-noon rocks,
they leave a trail
of sundried scales
that float
a thousand
question marks—
like rainbows,
adrift
on the
evening tide.

NATURAL GRACE

The frog pond
takes me in
and lets
my creature swim;
signaled
by the sun's slant
ripening the mud,
I know no lag
between inkling
and act.

Each leap
steps so rightly
with the larger pulse
that my time
and timelessness
are one.

MONARCH DAY

This is Monarch Day
at Ocean Point—
a natal convergence
signals flight;
flags the hour
for going south.

They are
a gathering
of fragility—
like heartbeats,
unmindful
of the odds,
yet built to last
miles and miles
of life storms.

REMEDIAL TEARS

The moon,
waxing full,
tugs at my substance
native to its pull:
springs tears
for the sake
of spilling them,
brings back
the primal ache
of urgent infancy,
unplugs a warm,
medicinal sea—
and the salt
of a cleansing
remedy
fixes me.

ODE TO AN EARTHEN VESSEL
Song of Myself

Spice-mustard
yellow bowl,
gem of the church bazaar,
how did you make it—
unchipped, thus far?

Straight from the forties,
you grace my bench
with fitness—
nooked between
nut basket and bead jar.

Not for cupboard
or restraint of shelves,
you're for garden dirt
and getting left
out in the rain

or sitting overnight
for sweeter gain:
the crackled red
scripture of
strawberries' stain.

UNEXPECTED GREEN

Sapling
in the parking lot
cracks the tar
like a paradox
blown just there
by a random wind.

Toe-nailed
into a shallow rift
stands
an unexpected green
like a parable
grown just there
to serve reason
for all unwise dreams
—just there—
simply for the surprise
of one short season.

OCTOBER FIRST

This Maine
morning
provides fog
as canvas for
those droplets
on the window pane;
bits of altered reality
slither down the glass.
Not one leaf falls
from the apple tree.

I am a bump on a log,
    struck dumb
      by simplicity.

FALL EQUINOX

It's primal clockwork
set off by October
and a spell of cold nights
that makes me pull back;
I sniff
and hunt for secrecy
or some narrow slot.
Not a cocoon
or darkness that gets
spring going again,
my sleep
will be a winter
of uneasy napping—
resisting
(with a million years between)—
the nagging
urge
to
dig.

JANUARY MORNING

The box stove barely
heats itself—and that
but food for the frigid room

The hearth holds nothing
for the feet; and boots
are posed with frozen yawns.

The poker, tipped on its
iron grip, is just more
cold to my gloveless hand.

The wood bin thins
to one last row, with
filling it, a chilling thought.

The morning light
shows through the pane,
aglow with fires of crystal frost.

SNOW PLOW FANTASY

Foretold
by a sequenced glow
of circling gold
that rings the tips
and flings shadows
of the drifts,
it tumbles a freshet of snow
and shakes our window;
—a lumbering UFO—
that comes down low
to show
the unknown
great power
of going slow.

OLD SAGE

I like being old—
for eccentricity
once disallowed
is permissible now
from one whose
iron will grows
transparent,
whose tongue
becomes docile;

whose mind
joins spirit,
widens the reach
of wing span
and whose eyes
stretch sight
to withstand
one last extreme—

the foreseeable
  Blind Leap

SOMETIMES THE MOON

Sometimes the moon
seems pinned
and halts mid-space
above the abstract
fringe of dreams
that crowd the lower air
with inter-laced,
free telecasts of sleep
and yet, the faultless
lunar clock
descends the west
unmarked by storms
of mortal thought;
and slower than time's
unhurried gold,
it hangs still
for sunrise.

MY FACE, A GLOBE

What random line
   of free will and courting,
   of wedded genes
   and lovely making
patterned this piece
   that now
   defines joy?

I, who carry
   the cheekbones
   from family albums
   and stare at this room
   with ancestral eyes,
am a resemblance—
   an age-mapped mirror:
   my face,
   a globe
   of many gifts.

AUTUMNAL PSALM

Golden rivers roar
in the sap stream
of one whose roots
have grown—
exposed by life storms—
prematurely old.
Psalms bow down the limbs
and tug at the heartwood.

A gravity of want
calls for the tongues
of prophets in your soul.

Speak for these times
as one who feels too much.
Make known
your sway of spirit—
written in growth rings—
as one season
turns
and
another begins.

DEPARTURE

Near the end,
an enlarged
love of life imparts
so clear and sharp a joy
as to break the heart
and sever the mind
cleanly from the soul

which then prepares
to simply float away
—mercifully—
without a sound
almost fleeing
the lump of clay
which is in fact
quite easily
dropped

and left behind.

HEBREWS 11:5
A Translation

A key is turned
in Heaven's door
for all those
pure of soul
who depart their clay
in a blink—
costumes thrown
in a pile
at curtain call;
who, when the second
bows are made,
have already
left the hall
and are elsewhere—
sweetly unaware
that they have
been transformed
from here
to
  There—

STACIE SMITH was born in Salem, Oregon. A fourth-generation Oregonian, she grew up in Eugene, in the Willamette Valley. She has been a visual artist for over fifty years. She was awarded a writer's residency at Playa Summer Lake, Oregon, in 2014. The following year she was granted a residency through Oregon State University's Spring Creek "Trillium Project." Her first book of poems, *Open Burning*, was self-published in 2016. *Meanwhile the Earth: Poems from Cougar Creek*, was published by Shanti Arts Publishing in 2018, followed by *Real News*, her third volume of poetry, in 2019. In June 2018 Stacie was invited to present her science-related poetry and art to the Yachats Academy of Arts and Sciences.

JUNE CAMPBELL ROSE was born in Boothbay Harbor, Maine. She has lived her entire life in that beautiful coastal region. She attended the University of Maine in Orono, where her poems were accepted for publication in a university collection. After graduation, while employed as a social worker, June moonlighted as a feature writer for the *Kennebec Journal.* As a young mother of three sons during the late sixties and seventies, June continued to write and seek publication in various periodicals, with some success. Her poems were included in two editions of Puddingstone Publications, a special feature of Boothbay Region's Annual Lincoln Arts Festival. Currently, June is gallery manager at the Boothbay Region Art Foundation, a nonprofit members' association. She is also a folk artist who produces fiber art, hand-made altered books, and mixed-media collage. She has been the organist at the East Boothbay Methodist Church for fifty years.

SHANTI ARTS

NATURE ▪ ART ▪ SPIRIT

Please visit us online
to browse our entire book catalog,
including poetry collections and fiction,
books on travel, nature, healing, art,
photography, and more.

Also take a look at our highly
regarded art and literary journal,
Still Point Arts Quarterly, which
may be downloaded for free.

www.shantiarts.com

www.ingramcontent.com/pod-product-compliance
Lightning Source LLC
Chambersburg PA
CBHW022108040426
42451CB00007B/177